Inspirational Leadership

Yusuf Biviji

Inspirational Leadership

Select thoughts and quotes for leaders

by

Yusuf Biviji

First edition, April 2012

ISBN 978-1463577902

Printed in the United States of America

Dedication

This book is dedicated to all those who have inspired someone in their lives.

Contents

Introduction

A business starts and ends with leadership. It is required at all stages for overall success. Every person is a potential leader - whether we have thousands, hundreds, tens, one, or even nobody officially reporting to us. Leadership is more a state of mind than an actual designation. It is a behavior. Countless stories can be told of how one person's contribution changed the world. The "power of one" transcends time and geography and gives us the unique ability to shape our future.

Leadership relies on several personal qualities that may not be visible but are very powerful. These include belief, courage, and a positive mindset. Good leadership comes not from learning a set of skills, but from genuine passion and real concern for others. People who love what they do and want to share that passion with others make the best leaders.

Management vs. Leadership–What Wins?
The general tendency is to place leadership on a higher pedestal than management. The reasons are many and the examples are powerful.

However, the two are often mutually exclusive. Leadership brings people together, making them part of a community that is contributing to something worthwhile; pure management focuses on providing answers and solving problems. Leadership requires courage, risk taking, and the ability to listen, trust, and learn from others; management brings order and helps systematize daily operations. Both are important and have their own value. But leadership is what moves the world. It is the emotional connection, the true change we seek, the force that propels us into the future.

This book reviews leadership qualities and recounts what great people have said about them. Although many of these quotes were stated in different contexts, they are still applicable today in the board-room, office cubicle, plant floor, or service center. These quotations should cause us to pause, refresh, and reflect on who we are and what we need to do. They remind us that we have to keep working diligently to build our abilities in spite of all the roadblocks we may face.

The chapter topics in this book flow from the foundations of leadership to the accomplishment of the end goal. It all starts with belief, ends with success and transcends into reflection. If we don't reflect on our successes, it's possible that what we call success may not be so. Finally, each chapter ends with a short anecdote or thought on the theme covered to drive home the point about the importance of each attribute.

Model Of How Leadership Attributes Build On Each Other:

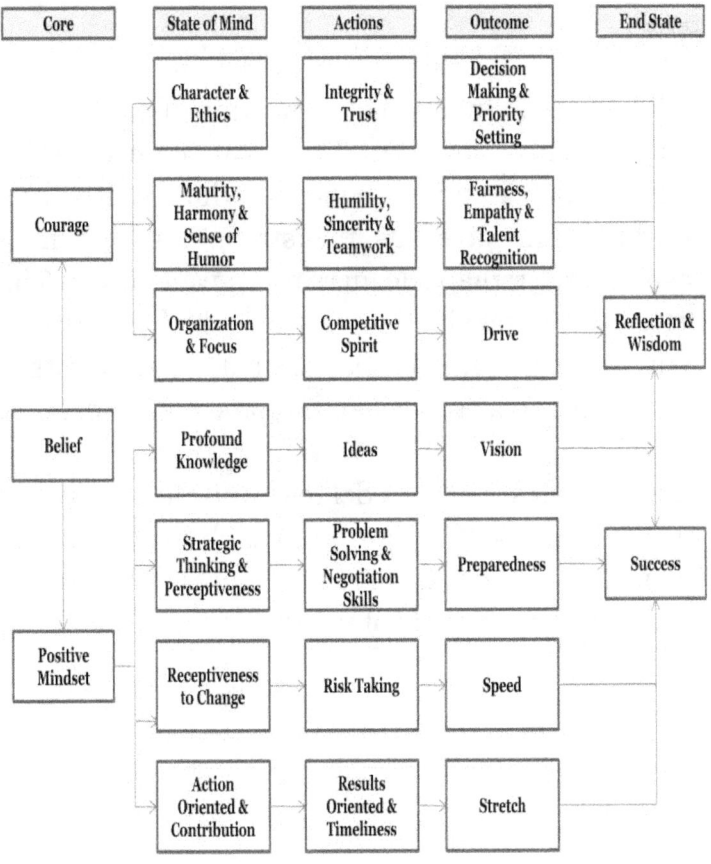

The model on the preceding page shows how different leadership attributes connect with each other. It is also the basis for the structure of this book.

Belief is the fountainhead from which flow courage and a positive mindset. These two core qualities enhance our ability to build on who we are. This internal state gives us the strength to act in a fashion that radiates leadership as we know it. The actions in turn yield results on which success is built. In the end, it is success that we seek with a reflection of if it truly yields happiness and wisdom.

The attributes in the model feed into each other but its comprehensive view outlines leadership. The inspiration to be the best in each area will drive us to achieve new heights of success.

1. Belief

If there is one quality that is apparent in a true leader, it is belief. This is a core leadership attribute, and a catalyst for all our behaviors, actions, and results.

Self-belief in our abilities makes us do things that will lead to success. If we give ourselves credit for our capabilities, others will too. Many times we underestimate what we can do and forget we are our own brand and should portray ourselves accordingly. If we don't, no one else will.

Think highly of yourself for the world takes you at your own estimate.

Anonymous

A half-hearted attempt at anything will never make us meet our objectives. It's all or nothing.

When you believe in a thing, believe in it all the way, implicitly and unquestionably.

Walt Disney

Belief and prayer are intertwined in many ways. Even if the act of prayer alone has a positive impact, it's worth the effort.

Who rises from prayer a better man, his prayer is answered.

George Meredith

Every person holds some beliefs. Even not having one is by definition, a belief.

Can atheists get insurance for acts of God?

Anonymous

Although such a claim may sound counterintuitive, one true benefit of belief is that it helps us keep an open mind and not be closed to new thoughts. It should enlighten us and give us an opportunity to grow. When we reject good ideas from others and let our narrow thinking dictate decision making, we risk missing opportunities that may never come back.

When you change the way you look at things, the things you look at change.

Wayne Dyer

Some businesses flourish on the belief that they can be the best, while others perish if all parties are concerned about only what they'll get out of it. Being focused on the numbers of the next quarterly statement or the next paycheck will do nothing for long term-success.

One person with a belief is equal to a force of 99 who have only interests.

John Stuart Mill

Being rock-solid in our belief will foster additional core leadership attributes such as courage and a positive mindset that are needed to be successful. These qualities do not automatically guarantee success but their presence is instrumental in leading to the desired goal.

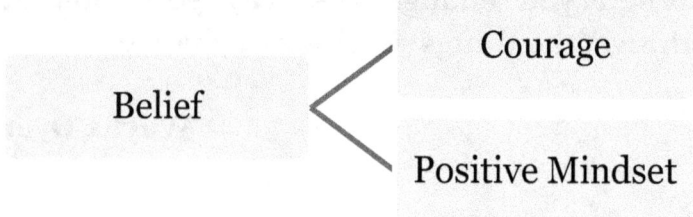

Belief is a very strong and powerful motivational force that serves as a guide through good and bad times. Walt Disney's story is a great example of how the core of a strong belief was translated into a flourishing business empire that meant something to him and also had an impact on the world. His vision for a better future was steeped in the belief that he could contribute to and be a part of change. He envisioned theme parks and the EPCOT Center in Orlando decades before they actually came to fruition. His vision of the ideal place resulted in the design and plan for the "experimental prototype community of tomorrow," a city where cultures of the world come together to show unity in diversity.

Belief in your abilities is the most powerful force for progress.

2. Courage

Nothing is accomplished without courage. "Against all odds" is a story recited very often. Our profound knowledge and progress is due to the courage of thought leaders from the present and past. We have it in our DNA but it may not always be dominant. Sometimes it needs some spurring and the right environment to get it going.

It is not life that matters but the courage we bring to it.

Horace Walpole

Our abilities often lie in our self-concept. If we show the courage to rise and deliver, the odds of success increase tremendously.

Whether you think you can, or that you can't, you are right.

Henry Ford

If we think that we don't possess the same capabilities as others who are successful, then we will rightfully have thought so. Our ability is dictated by how much we believe and the courage we have to do things.

Argue for your limitations and sure enough, they're yours.

Richard Bach

The courage to do something often depends on our perception of the world around us. If an action results in what we deem as failure, we tend not to proceed further. This perception breeds inaction and leads to greater failure. We do not realize that we could be learning a lot unconsciously while the world hands us our certification of non-performance.

When we think we fail, we are often very near success.

Anonymous

Not all attempts lead to the desired state. Failure is common and occurs quite often. A person needs courage to know that even if success is never realized, it's still worth pushing forward and trying our best. Sometimes it may take generations to observe true change.

It is better to have fought and spent your courage, missing all the applause, than to have lived in smug content and never ventured a cause.

Edgar Guest

The key is not to give up on courage. The more it's cultivated, the more we have in reserve. It is the gift that never stops giving.

Courage is like a muscle. We strengthen it with use.

Ruth Gordon

Courage is a bit antithetical to planning. A planner needs to predict what's coming and to prepare for it. With raw courage, one intelligently takes on a challenge without pre-calculating every move.

Courage can't see around corners, but goes around them anyway.

Mignon McLaughlin

Sometimes we can't let go of apprehension, but without doing so, it's not possible to find opportunities. Positively challenging established thoughts may lead to great ideas.

You cannot discover new oceans unless you have the courage to lose sight of the shore.

Anonymous

Courage builds character, ethical values, maturity, harmony, a sense of humor, and focus. These attributes develop the self and in-turn spawn many other traits that are vital to leadership.

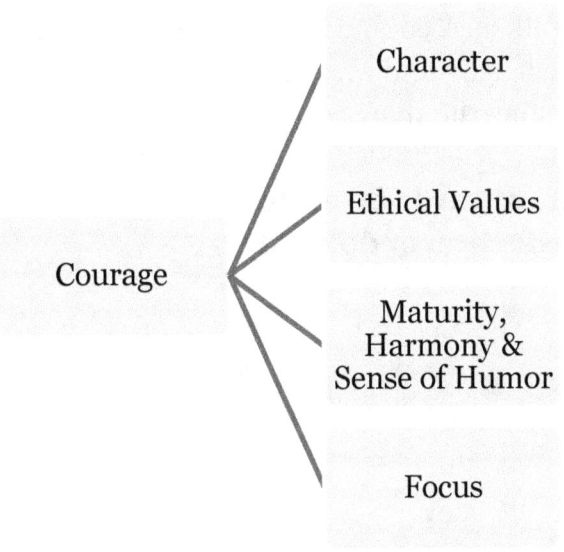

Courage requires immense self-determination. Whether something is worth doing or not depends on one's point of view and the courage to do it. This trait is best seen in someone who starts a small business. There are many who may be subject-matter experts in their fields but who prefer the shelter of a steady income over the risk of starting something new with no guarantee of cash-flow for a while. Those who have decided to start their own ventures have done so more out of pure courage than of having an in-depth knowledge of all the intricacies of the business.

Not all succeed, but many do and those with only knowledge and no courage are left behind watching the show.

The reward of a courageous act is the satisfaction of doing it.

3. Positive Mindset

Another offshoot of strong belief is a positive mindset that will make us behave in ways leading to our goals. Just as negativity is contagious, so is positivity. It can overcome great obstacles and problems. Life at the workplace can be stressful and hectic. The constant barrage of requirements can lead to reduced morale. In these situations, a positive attitude can help put things back in perspective for long-term objectives.

Most people are about as happy as they make up their mind to be.

Abraham Lincoln

A leader can calm frayed nerves and help teams improve performance by supporting their actions. Having the leader's backing motivates people to deliver beyond basic expectations.

One of the toughest things in the world is a mind filled with hope.

Norman V. Peale

Hope will soon fade if it is not backed with concrete action. Work that yields good results will motivate. Progress is a great vitamin for a positive mindset.

One of the greatest sources of energy is having pride in what you do.

Anonymous

Our intrinsic disposition will dictate if we want to make the best of every situation. Things are not always fair or easy. Looking at the "bright side" is something that has worked and will continue to do so.

Those who wish to sing always find a song.

Anonymous

Work is work only if it is a chore. Mary Poppins famously said in the 1967 Disney movie, "If you find the fun, the job's a game; and every task you undertake becomes a piece of cake." Being stuck in a job you hate is like going to prison every day.

Find something you love to do and you'll never have to work a day in your life.

Harvey Mackay

If we would keep smiling and work toward our goals, everyday would be a lot more fun. A positive attitude is reflected in our body language.

You cannot control the contours of your face, but you can control its expression.

Anonymous

Nothing will always go right or our way. When something goes wrong, treat it as a learning experience. Don't make the same mistakes twice.

Never regret. If it's good, it's wonderful. If it's bad, it's experience.

Victoria Holt

Every situation has a "win" and a "lose." Our failures as well as our successes can serve us well in ways we cannot see in the short-term.

Always look at what you have left. Never look at what you have lost.

Robert H. Schuller

Belief coupled with a positive attitude sets the stage for gaining profound knowledge, strategic thinking, being receptive to change, and being action oriented. Just like the outcomes of courage, the above attributes do not give us a free pass to success. They get us ready to use our abilities in the best possible manner.

No one evokes more admiration for a positive mindset than Helen Keller. Her accomplishments defied all logic, yet she made them seem so easy. When she said that "So much has been given to me; I have no time to ponder over that which has been denied," her words brought out the core of her thought process.

A positive frame of mind can make big problems seem small.

4. Character and Ethics

Character is the material people and companies are made of. It is built out of each individual's framework of belief and courage. It helps develop integrity, trust, and decision making. It also determines the ultimate path of a person or an organization.

Who you are has a whole lot to do with what you think about most of the time.

Anonymous

One thing leads to another and small actions become larger deeds. We need to nip the negativities in the bud lest they get out of control.

Watch your thoughts; they become words.
Watch your words; they become actions.
Watch your actions; they become habits.
Watch your habits; they become character.
Watch your character; it becomes your destiny.

Frank Outlaw

Character stands the test of time. We have seen brilliant people accomplish great things but we have also seen them get into a whole lot of trouble. Brilliance and strength without character is like waging a mighty war without a purpose.

Ability may get you to the top but it takes character to keep you there.

John Wooden

Our behavior dictates who we are and it will determine what we become. Pretending to be different will only weaken us to the point that we may succumb to temptations.

Act the way you'd like to be and soon you'll be the way you act.

George W. Crane

At times, we crumble under pressures of the moment and compromise our character.

When I let go of what I am, I become what I might be.

Lao Tzu

Character is the hallmark of leadership. It is the source of inspiration to keep going on a certain path and not compromising on basic values.

Although genius always commands admiration,
Character most secures respect.
While the former is admired;
The latter is followed.

Samuel Smiles

We should watch what we say for while we judge others, they will be judging us.

You never reveal your character more vividly than when portraying the character of another.

Anonymous

There isn't much out there besides our inbuilt mechanism to guide us to make sound decisions and distinguish right from wrong.

Nearly all can stand adversity, but if you want to test someone's character, give them power.

Abraham Lincoln

All people and businesses operate by their own code of ethics. These differ by country, region, and culture. What could be legal in many places might be unethical, and thus not an act that a person or an organization would want their name attached to. Very often when an individual or a corporation is caught in an unethical act, their first instinct is to hide it and lie about the facts. Thus, an unethical act is followed-up by another, getting one deeper into trouble.

The shame is in the crime, not in the punishment.

Voltaire

Ethics are intrinsic and self-developed. They give us a path to move ahead with conviction while being sensitive to others. Laws can merely teach rules but it is up to each one of us to have a mental compass of right and wrong. Belief and courage will lend themselves to developing a strong sense of ethics.

Work out your own salvation. Do not depend on others.

Buddha

The values a person possesses often turns out to be the roadmap for his or her future.

It is our choices that show what we truly are, far more than our abilities.

J. K. Rowling

Common-sense should dictate our ethical values. Explanations and rationalizations may often complicate something that should be very simple.

When I do good, I feel good. When I do bad, I feel bad. And that's my religion.

Abraham Lincoln

Character and ethics are core attributes that lead to integrity and trust. These are the ingredients for sound decision making.

Character & Ethics Integrity & Trust

J.K. Rowling, the author of the Harry Potter series, brought out the point of making the right choices as a determining factor of each person's ethical values. The abilities of the main villain, Voldemort, and that of Harry Potter were very similar in nature. Both had the same powers. However, one chose to misuse them while the other persevered to harness them for the larger good. With new scientific breakthroughs, it is easy to imagine how inventions and abilities can be misdirected to satisfy greed. That is why ethical values should factor into our decision making process.

There are some things we cannot select, but what we can, we should choose wisely.

5. Maturity, Harmony, and Sense of Humor

Maturity is an often overlooked leadership attribute. Someone could have all the other attributes combined but if he or she lacks maturity, the person would fail to understand some very important pieces of the business or the human effort. In that sense, maturity stands alone. It's a difficult trait to build; you either have it, or you don't. With that said, maturity should not be confused with age. Age lends experience; not maturity.

You are young only once, but you can be immature indefinitely.

Oscar Wilde

Sometimes it takes understanding a paradox in order to realize bigger and better things.

To live with fear and not be afraid is the final test of maturity.

Edwards Weeks

Maturity could lead to finding harmony among us. Harmony is all about seeking a common ground, reducing friction, and getting the job done. It abhors conflict and confrontation and sees them as distractions in reaching the end goal. We are continually faced with divisiveness in terms of race, religion, ethnicity, national origin, or even with non-physical attributes such as personalities and temperament. Cohesiveness and harmony are a challenge for us all.

We have learned to fly in the air like birds and to swim in the sea like fish. But we have not learned the simple act of living together.

Martin Luther King

Change is constant but with it comes discord, anxiety, and a feeling of unsettledness. Bringing in maturity and harmony will reduce these tensions and make the process of change smoother. For most, well managed change is only found in fairy tales.

The art of progress is to preserve order amid change and to preserve change amid order.

Warren Wiersbe

"Never waste a good crisis," or so we have heard. It is always in the midst of negativities that we must find positives.

Three Rules of Work: Out of clutter find simplicity; from discord find harmony; in the middle of difficulty lies opportunity.

Albert Einstein

Happiness means a lot of things to different people, but one way to define it is in the context of perfect harmony.

Happiness is when what you think, what you say, and what you do are in harmony.

M. K. Gandhi

Harmony does not need perfection. We can find peace anywhere.

Serenity is not freedom from the storm, but calmness within the storm.

Anonymous

Anger allows us to express ourselves for a few seconds and then makes us remorseful for years to come. Controlling anger prevents discord and removes regret.

If you can suppress a moment of anger, you can prevent a day of sorrow.

R. W. Emerson

Someone with maturity should also have a keen sense of humor. It is one of the greatest assets of an individual. Humor helps put things in perspective and serves as a defense mechanism when things are not going too well.

It's better to laugh at life than to lament over it.

Seneca

It's difficult to find humor when we are in the middle of fixing problems or finding solutions. We usually see the funny side later and laugh about it then. If we were to see the humor of a situation while it is unfolding, we would be able to get through it with much less stress.

There is a humorous side to every situation. The challenge is to find it.

George Carlin

Seeing the lighter side and looking at the big picture helps us to navigate the waters better and get through problems faster. Just dwelling on the size of the issues could consume us and prevent us from focusing to find innovative solutions. Good leaders know that and never allow themselves to be overwhelmed to the extent that it impacts their ability to lead.

Were it not for my little jokes, I could not bear the burdens of this office.

Abraham Lincoln

Maturity, harmony, and a sense of humor lead to humility, sincerity, and teamwork.

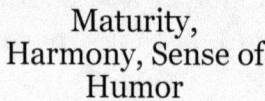

Maturity, Harmony, Sense of Humor → Humility, Sincerity, Teamwork

Can't we all just live together? John Lennon, Gandhi, and Martin Luther King Jr., all propagated peace, but the world has trouble following it. The maturity to live in harmony would make lives better and enjoyable. It's easy to hate but to love takes refinement.

Having a sense of humor is also a sign of maturity. It prevents us from getting caught in the minutia. We should look at the intent and results and not the exact way we think something should be done. In many situations, if working from home can accomplish more, then by all means we should do it. This would not only improve employee morale, but also help save the planet by depleting less of its resources. Maturity also involves not fretting too much about getting credit for work done. Facts will be facts and good performance will always show.

Maturity is a subtle trait but yields great results.

6. Organization and Focus

Planning an endeavor requires a keen focus on what needs to be accomplished and how, through the organization of thought and action. Embarking on a project without fully defining the plan and not considering potential failures could lead to wasted effort.

To climb steep hills requires slow pace at first.

William Shakespeare

Our focus should be on what we need to accomplish next. As we plan and organize our actions, we should remember that the world around us may not know what we are working on and will continue to view us based on what we have done in the past. Even though companies work toward innovating new solutions, their customers and competitors view them based on past performance. This perception is important to remember since it impacts marketing, public relations, and communications.

We judge ourselves by what we feel capable of doing; others judge us by what we have done.

Henry Longfellow

The institutionalization of organization and focus creates not just one-time success, but a consistent delivery of quality. What takes conscious effort at first becomes a way of life and a standard for everyone to follow.

We are what we repeatedly do. Excellence then, is not an act, but a habit.

Aristotle

Motivation is intrinsic in nature and when things do not go well, this internal clock that pushes us to keep moving forward slows down, or even stops. At this point, giving up becomes the best option, because it is the easiest one. If we were to view our setbacks as just bumps along the way and approach them with zeal, they could be the stepping stones for the future.

One of the most common causes of failure is the habit of quitting when one is overtaken by temporary defeat. Every person is guilty of this mistake at one time or another.

Napoleon Hill

Success is seen when there is commitment to a purpose and the courage to take action. The combination of these two inputs forms a volatile mixture that begins the process of making a dream into reality.

Once you make a decision, the universe conspires to make it happen.

Ralph Waldo Emerson

All this discourse about organization and focus would suggest that all we need is a solid plan. After acknowledging its importance, it is good to remember that the pendulum should not swing excessively on either side. Ideas and ingenuity come from other non-work situations such as play, relaxation, and conversation. We just need to keep our eyes and minds open.

I like nonsense. It wakes up the brain cells.

Dr. Seuss

Organization and focus lead to the enhanced ability to compete and improve performance by solving problems. This increases the drive to deliver and succeed.

Organization & Focus Competitive Spirit

The "Five Guys" fast food franchise is an excellent example of organization and focus. The chain is built around a few core values of quality, efficiency, value, and cleanliness. You can't order milk shakes or salads, and you cannot get the latest action figures there. What you can get, though, are fresh ingredients of the highest quality, quick service, a well- maintained clean setting, and reasonable pricing- with free peanuts!

The franchise focuses on this simple concept of a few very important ideas, delivered consistently in a friendly atmosphere.

Focus on your strengths and do them well.

7. Profound Knowledge

Profound knowledge is the crucible for ideas and for a vision of the future. Without it there is little that can be accomplished. One needs to invest in knowledge to dream big. Our aspirations don't become reality by accident.

The most incomprehensible thing about the world is that it is comprehensible.

Albert Einstein

Knowledge should be sought from all sources; even from history. It's not just for academicians.

The farther backward you can look, the farther forward you are likely to see.

Winston Churchill

Every time we turn to look back, we find a business entity missing, replaced by another new, growing, dynamic company. Simple lessons from the past can prove to be very valuable for the future. Companies perish because they deviate from what made them great in the first place.

Those who forget history are condemned to repeat it.

Anonymous

Our knowledge-base has grown exponentially over the years and now it's impossible to learn everything. So, as we prioritize our learning, we should focus on the significant. Plan to be the subject matter expert in some areas while gaining at least a high-level knowledge in others. If we continue to learn how things work outside our field of expertise, it will enable us to ask the right questions when dealing with experts from other areas.

A great manager knows everything of something and something of everything.

Anonymous

What we consider profound knowledge may or may not mean much when it comes to learning greater realities. Our knowledge may be miniscule in comparison to what we don't know. If we keep working to expand our horizon of understanding, we will be able to realize the scope of everything someday.

We don't know a millionth of one percent about anything.

Thomas Edison

Our progress today is based on challenging wrong notions of the past. The courage and zeal to learn has brought us to where we are today. As long as this endeavor continues, we will continue to expand our horizons.

To be conscious that you are ignorant is a great step to knowledge.

Benjamin Disraeli

Profound knowledge is built on the premise of constant learning. As we learn and discover, we will be able to build the tower of knowledge and ability.

I am always doing that which I cannot do, in order that I may learn how to do it.

Pablo Picasso

The more we learn, the more we realize how little we know. That sounds paradoxical but the realization of how little we know comes with deep knowledge. In large organizations, very few individuals usually understand how the entire business works from the ground-up. Henry Ford once remarked that even if everything he had set-up were destroyed, he would be able to recreate it all. He was an exception who comprehended all working parts of his business.

It takes considerable knowledge just to realize the extent of your own ignorance.

Thomas Sowell

Profound knowledge is the seed for ideation. Ideas lead to creating the vision for the future.

When Isaac Newton was old, a friend asked him if he was proud and gratified to know that he had penetrated so deeply into the knowledge of nature's laws. Newton replied by saying that far from feeling proud, he felt like a child who had found a few bright-colored shells and pebbles, while the vast ocean of truth stretched unknown and unexplored before his eager fingers. This story shows that profound knowledge is a thirst that will continue to push us to explore and learn, but the journey is not at all over.

Strive to maximize learning, but realize we may only be scratching the surface.

8. Strategic Thinking and Perceptiveness

Strategy allows us to see an opportunity where others may see complexity. It is a process of getting us prepared for the future. Strategic thinking helps businesses grow and makes life better. It's the right career choice, the perfect price point, or the dream product. Sometimes it is no action at all, but done with a conscious frame of mind.

Strategic thinking can help us see value even though it may not be apparent to all. This in turn helps us make decisions that could yield great dividends, or in the case of wrong decisions, great losses.

There is no comparison between that which is lost by not succeeding and that which is lost by not trying.

Francis Bacon

The strategy behind innovation is developing new products and services that people love. Customers see value when a certain need is fulfilled, for example, easy access to information. Those who were first in this quest have seen tremendous gains in the marketplace by developing and selling the 'gotta have it' products.

If you have something you can't do without, you don't own it; it owns you.

Albert Schweitzer

Many new technology companies have a large proportion of employees from the younger generation. Their strategy is to use high-tech skills taught in college to develop the latest products. This method of looking at things from only one point of view could miss out on some obvious gaps. Older folks too are a great talent bank and their skills should not be ignored.

Age is opportunity no less than youth itself, though in another dress.

Anonymous

Let's choose our battles, or we'll be fighting all day. Decide where we need to spend our energy and what will yield the most dividends. Strategy is another word for prioritization. It is finding an opportunity and making good decisions. Although strategy might indicate that a certain action may have a huge upside, the wisdom of performing the action should always be questioned.

The art of being wise is the art of knowing what to overlook.

William James

Perceptiveness is a gift, while strategy is a learned skill. One can argue this point, but being perceptive goes beyond strategy. It is the ability to know what's going to happen next without any concrete data. It also allows a person to feel what others are thinking, thus adding that variable in future communications and decision making.

The greatest of faults, I should say, is to be conscious of none.

Thomas Carlyle

We can use the ability of being perceptive to our advantage by realizing what others think of us and modifying the way we portray ourselves with the right image. Perceptiveness should be mixed with confidence. That's when people will listen.

To establish oneself in the world one has to do all one can to appear established.

Anonymous

Understanding how others feel gives us unique insight into their thinking. Soon it becomes apparent that the ideal state we all strive for is never here but always in the future. There is no need to accomplish all our goals at once. That's why we have the concept of time.

Happiness is knowing that you do not necessarily require happiness.

William Saroyan

Perceptiveness is innate and can be leveraged to make wise decisions. Understanding others adds a new dimension to decision making with well-rounded sensitivity. Marketing campaigns that lack this feature end up hurting one group or another and the creators of the campaigns see their efforts backfire.

A mix of strategy and perceptiveness helps prepare for the ups and downs of the future, which in turn enables us to proactively fix problems and negotiate the best solutions.

Strategy & Perceptiveness Problem Solving and Negotiation Skills

It is important to look for opportunities and make decisions to create value. The ability to do so is not very common. Socrates, as the story goes, used to ask all his potential students to look into a pond of still water and tell him what they saw. The ones who waited for a while and saw the fish swimming were accepted, while those who were quick to point to their own reflection were not admitted.

Strategic thinking involves looking beyond what is apparent.

9. Receptiveness to Change and Listening Skills

Change is inevitable. A new boss, an organizational realignment, a promotion, or even a demotion; it's all around us. Each day brings with it something different.

Society, too, demands change every now and then. From politics to cultural preferences, we see how new ideas take shape and soon become accepted. We as individuals should not just be adaptable to change, but also be agents of one.

Whenever you find that you are on the side of the majority, it is time to reform.

Mark Twain

Another way to look at change is to have the ability to move-on. Things happen, but if we stay stuck in the past, our future will not be any different. It's important to look forward to new ventures and not re-open closed chapters.

To be wronged is nothing unless you continue to remember it.

Confucius

Change does not necessarily impact oneself only. It is something that can be used to realize someone else's potential. Leaders should use it to benefit others.

Leadership is the art of changing a group from what it is into what it can be.

Anonymous

Although change is everywhere, some basic principles remain the same. Core values should and will continue to stay constant. They should dominate our thinking and decision making.

The more things change, the more they remain the same.

Anonymous

People are not often receptive to change because they do not listen. When we listen, we open our minds to the other person's point of view and begin seeing things in a different light. This prepares us for change, and makes us a part of it.

Of all the leadership skills, listening is the least talked about. Maybe it is mentioned often, but nobody listens! Listening does not just mean talking less. It means understanding others, walking in their shoes and being ready to accept change.

Listening is very inexpensive. Not listening could be very costly.

Tom Brewer

In meetings at the workplace, many times individuals talk to feel that they are adding value. In such situations, nobody's listening while everybody is concentrating on what they are going to say next. When everyone talks, the overall agenda becomes secondary. We need to understand first and talk later.

The most valuable of all talents is never using two words when one will do.

Thomas Jefferson

Listening as a form of verbal communication is counter-intuitive but if looked at holistically, body language, listening, and speaking all combined constitutes verbal communication. If our input adds more value, only then is there any reason to consume air waves.

Don't talk unless you can improve the silence.

Anonymous

Only by being receptive to other people's points of view can we think of taking measured risks to accomplish goals. The right risks help speed things up which could put us on the fast-track to success.

Receptiveness to Change & Listening Skills Risk taking

Change is not easy and does not come without its share of trials and tribulations. The struggles we go through during times of change are often needed for our very survival. We see this in nature too, and the following story aptly drives home the point:

A biology teacher was demonstrating to her class how a caterpillar turns into a butterfly. She told the students that in the next couple of hours, the butterfly would try to come out of the cocoon. Before leaving, she also cautioned that no one should help the butterfly.

As the students waited, they saw the butterfly struggle to get out of the cocoon. Soon they took pity on it and, against the advice of their teacher, decided to help it out. They broke the cocoon to help the butterfly. Shortly after coming out, the butterfly died.

In an attempt to help, the students had actually accomplished the opposite. Nature needs the butterfly to work hard to come out. This action helps develop and strengthen its wings. When deprived of this opportunity, the butterfly was not strong enough to survive. Change needs struggle and perseverance. It is part of the process.

Listening to your customers is required if you want to improve in business. Companies that do not listen will not be around for too long. Some businesses make it a habit to get customer feedback and use it as a source of information to improve their processes. One such firm is Living Social, the online coupon site. For every deal that is purchased, the buyer is asked for a "thumbs up" or a "thumbs down." The feedback received helps the company provide better offerings in the future.

Listen and change.

10. Action Oriented

Inertia; this universal law prevents us from doing a lot of good things. Some people call it laziness too. We do not have to wait for all the stars to align before taking the first step. The additive nature of small actions can lead to great accomplishments. Actions speak louder than words.

You cannot build a reputation on what you are going to do.

Henry Ford

It's all in the thought! Well, not really.

Small deeds done are better than great deeds planned.

Anonymous

The main reason for lack of action is the fear of taking on something that may fail. If our commitment to an idea is weak, action will not follow. It takes motivation to get things going.

Action springs not from thought, but from a readiness for responsibility.

Dietrich Bonhoeffer

Many people do not start a new venture because they believe their input will not make a difference in what is already being done. Why work on a better sports drink when you have multi-national companies spending tremendous resources to develop something better? What most people do not realize is that many of the best innovations come not from big companies, but from individuals motivated to do something new.

Act as if what you do makes a difference. It does.

William James

The key to success is action. Action does not only mean working. It's a lot more. It is the ability to take ourselves to the next level.

Do more than belong: participate

Do more than care: help
Do more than believe: practice
Do more than be fair: be kind
Do more than forgive: forget
Do more than dream: work

William Arthur Ward

Do not wait for that perfect moment to begin something because if we do, we'll be waiting for a long time. Have the belief and the proper mindset to act decisively right away.

To change one's life, start immediately. Do it flamboyantly. No exceptions.

William James

Instead of aimlessly whiling away time without any intent or purpose, we should believe in ourselves, have a positive attitude, and start working. One thing will lead to another and opportunity will present itself.

The tragedy of life is not that it ends so soon but that we wait so long to begin it.

W. M. Lewis

Action is based on intent. If someone does not want to act, he or she will find every reason in the book not to, while those who want to will open doors even when none exist.

A person who wants to do something will find a way;
A person who doesn't will find an excuse.

Stephen Doley

Procrastination is the thief of time! Act before it's too late! We have heard these words several times but do not heed them when we need to.

Great thoughts converted to practice will become great accomplishments.

William Hazlitt

Haste is waste. Action without thought is like jumping off a cliff hoping to make a soft landing. In retrospect, it will not be a good decision.

One of the greatest disadvantages of hurry is that it takes such a long time.

G. K. Chesterton

Contribution is the ability to do our part in the big scheme of things, without trying to overtake the entire project. Movies and history focus on individual heroes. We have also read stories of a single leader who changes everything. That's what we are taught and believe in. However, are we going to wait for that golden opportunity to shape the outcome or just begin with something today?

We can do no great things, only small things with great love.

Mother Teresa

Most problems are overwhelming, but taking one small step at a time could add up and compound to giant leaps in the future.

I am one, but still I am one;
I cannot do everything, but still I can do something;
And just because I cannot do everything,
I will not refuse to do the something that I can do.

Helen Keller

And then, there is the question of who should be recognized for work done-the person who thought of the idea, the one who started working on it, or the one who completed it? Finally, what about those who maintained a low profile and just focused on getting the job done?

It is amazing what you can accomplish if you do not care who gets the credit.

Harry S. Truman

Action and contribution are the heart of all business. These qualities yield results and if done well, would be timely too. One of the gains of being action oriented is to eventually extend basic results into something more that exceed expectations.

Action-oriented individuals do not accept things the way they are, but strive to improve them. If Reed Hastings, the creator of Nexflix, had settled for paying Blockbuster's late fees and not done anything about it, he would have missed a huge business opportunity. But that was not the case. He made the decision to start a small-scale movie-rental business in his own neighborhood with two marketing tools: no late fees and movies delivered to your doorstep. Blockbuster did not offer either of these benefits, so Hastings' venture was an instant hit. A lot of people had been upset with late fees, but the one who took action rather than simply complaining, used his dissatisfaction to come out ahead.

Use action as a tool to seize opportunities, not as an outlet to create friction.

11. Integrity and Trust

Character breeds integrity and trust. It's not possible to have *some* integrity. Either you have it or you don't. Integrity is internal; it's something we possess. Trust is external; it's something we build over time.

Integrity is doing the right thing even if nobody is watching.

Jim Stovall

Beliefs, courage, and character all build integrity. It's the result of painstaking efforts to be the best we can.

Don't worry so much about your self-esteem. Worry more about your character. Integrity is its own reward.

Dr. Laura Schlessinger

Honesty is a quality that builds trust. It is a result of integrity. It takes time to build a reputation of honesty but just one error in judgment to lose it.

Integrity is telling myself the truth. Honesty is telling the truth to other people.

Spencer Johnson

Integrity is not just a feel good, self righteous state, but also a business tool. Many have found great fortune by sporting the integrity badge and putting the customer's mind at ease. Even retailers who are perceived to have integrity may attract more customers based on that fact alone.

The most important persuasion tool you have in your entire arsenal is integrity.

Zig Ziglar

A great leader should have the ability to gain the trust of others as well as create it within an organization. Trust is usually difficult to build and easy to break. It plays an important part in the success of a business. Once established, it can be used as a tool to get things done efficiently, thus reducing costs. Its absence creates the need for increased bureaucracy and the necessity to prove every point.

There are two ways in which trust can be built within an organization. One is at a personal level and the other is at the organizational level. The first one deals with creating it in our day-to-day behavior, for others to see. This can be accomplished by maintaining consistency in work habits, communicating effectively, developing strong subject-matter knowledge, and standing up for the ideals we believe in.

The organizational-level trust involves creating an identity for the company, delivering consistent messages about the business and being fair in the way employees are treated. Trust is a great motivational force and something any business should be proud of.

Yearn to understand first and to be understood second.

Beca Allen

Trust does not come without work. It takes conscious effort to make sure that those we deal with fully understand us and are willing to place their good faith in us.

Blessed are those who can give without remembering and take without forgetting.

Elizabeth Bibesco

Trust cannot be present without honesty. In fact, honesty is the root that nourishes the tree of trust.

Make yourself an honest person and then you will be sure there is one less rascal in the world.

Thomas Carlyle

Do things confidently. We won't always succeed, but confidence is contagious, so those around us will believe in our conviction and continue with our mission. Rationalizing everything could be viewed as a sign of weakness. Do what we have to do with the right spirit.

Never explain your actions. Your friends don't need it and your adversaries won't believe you anyway.

Anonymous

Trust is built over time. It is a process that slowly comes to fruition. Once it is established, trivial events should not be the reason for trust to erode. It should be a solid bond between two parties which withstands obstacles.

Be slow to fall into friendship but, when you are in, continue firm and constant.

Socrates

Trust has to be built on truth. A lie has a funny way of finding itself in the limelight.

If you tell the truth, you don't have to remember anything.

Mark Twain

From integrity and trust stem the ability to make sound decisions and set priorities.

Once during a busy time when Woodrow Wilson's secretary suggested a game of golf, the President replied, "My boss won't let me do it." "Your boss?" questioned the secretary, wondering who could have such powers over the chief executive of the United States. "Yes, I have a conscience and that is my boss," said the President. "It drives me to the task and it will not let me accept the tempting invitation."

You are the only guard of your integrity.

12. Humility, Sincerity, and Teamwork

A successful leader needs to understand the importance of humility. Arrogance works in the short run but will hinder long term progress. It impacts decision making and judgment. Humility, on the other hand, is the secret to seeing the world differently. It's a natural gift for some, but the ones who consciously learn about it need to use it with care.

Humility is a strange thing. The minute you think you've got it, you've lost it.

La Rochefoucauld

It's possible not to have humility but think you do. A lot of arrogant folks will have a self image of being humble. The beholder always knows, though.

What the world needs is more geniuses with humility - there are so few of us left.

Oscar Levant

Humility is often confused with weakness or a lack of self-esteem. It is quite different from either. It's actually a strength, something built out of belief, courage and maturity. For many, it comes late in life, after the arrogance of youth has proven to be hollow.

Life is a long lesson in humility.

James Matthew Barrie

Humility is the perfect attribute to use to prevent getting disheartened or dejected. Pride takes its toll, but humility stands as a guard, protecting from failure.

Humility is the only certain defense against humiliation.

Anonymous

The end objective of building leadership qualities is to be meaningfully successful. Humility is a stepping stone in that direction.

When pride comes, then comes disgrace, but with humility comes wisdom

The Bible

We don't spend enough time thinking about what we have. We take things for granted and seldom realize their importance until they are taken away. Good health, a family, a roof over our heads, food and water; what would we do without them?

A single grateful thought is the most complete prayer.

Gotthold Lessing

Pride is the opposite of humility. It is the root-cause of a lot of wars and mis-trust. Having the need to feel important could manifest itself as pride but could actually be due to a deep-seated feeling of insecurity. Being secure in our thoughts leads to humility and harmony. A lot of waste is avoided.

Half of the harm that is done in the world is due to people who want to feel important.

T. S. Eliot

Sincerity is another form of humility. Showing sincerity in our words and deeds indicates that we care and will do our best without malice. It's truly appreciated by the recipient when sincerity is interpreted to be genuine. When we feel that someone has done a great job, it is best to seize the moment and offer sincere appreciation. If we don't we lose an opportunity that may never come again.

Feeling gratitude and not expressing it is like wrapping a present and not giving it.

William Arthur Ward

The key to sincerity is genuineness. If someone senses that appreciation offered is either done with ridicule or as a chore, it will lose its effect or will even backfire.

The secret to success is sincerity. Once you can fake that you've got it made.

Anonymous

Be careful with praise. Too much of it will make sincere appreciation lose its efficacy. A measured use will have more effect.

People ask for criticism but they only want praise.

Somerset Maugham

A false show of being sincere will become apparent very quickly with body language and other non-verbal cues. Be genuine and gain the admiration of others.

When we try to make an impression, that's exactly the impression we make.

Anonymous

Teamwork is the glue that gets people together and delivers more than the sum of the individuals. It needs a common purpose and shared motivation. A team can be successful when learning and discovering without fear of penalty. If a group is told to do things but not given the reasons for doing so, teamwork will not flourish.

I am always willing to learn; however, I do not always like to be taught.

Winston Churchill

Teamwork wins when humility and fair behavior dominate thought and action. These things matter equally in kindergarten as well as the boardroom.

Good manners and soft words have brought many a difficult thing to pass.

Aesop

Teams succeed not with their size but with their sense of mission. Large teams in fact may have a problem of logistics and co-ordination.

What counts is not necessarily the size of the dog in the fight; it's the size of the fight in the dog.

Dwight D. Eisenhower

When our attributes work in concert, productivity improves.

Ability is what you're capable of doing. Motivation determines what you do. Attitude determines how well you do it.

Lou Holtz

Teamwork takes the "I" out of the equation and puts the "us" in front. It makes the output of the team add up to more than the sum of its individuals.

It is literally true that you can succeed best and quickest by helping others to succeed.

Napoleon Hill

Humility, sincerity, and teamwork lead to the acts of showing empathy, recognizing talent, and being fair to others.

Humility, Sincerity & Teamwork   Fairness, Empathy & Recognize Talent

At a school reunion, a group of highly established, career-oriented alumni got together with one of their old teachers. The conversation soon turned to long work hours and associated stress and health issues. Offering her students coffee, the teacher went to the kitchen and returned with a large container of the beverage and an assortment of cups: porcelain, plastic, glass; crystal; some were plain looking, some elegant and expensive.

When all the students had helped themselves to coffee, the teacher said that all the nice-looking cups were taken, leaving behind the plain and cheap ones. Although it is normal for one to want the best for themselves, that could also be the source of all the stress and problems. "What you really wanted," she observed, "was coffee, not the cup. Yet, you consciously selected the best ones and were also eyeing each other's cups."

Humility teaches you to focus on the coffee and not the cup. "Life is the coffee," the teacher told her former students, "and career, jobs, money, house, cars, etc. are the cups. They are just the tools to hold and contain life. Sometimes, by concentrating only on the cup, we fail to enjoy the coffee."

Humility is being sincere and true to oneself and to the world.

13. Competitive Spirit

Competitiveness strives for first place. It's not good to be the second. Go for the gold and do what it takes to get there. We know that others are working hard, so our objective should be to out-smart and out-work them to be at the top.

Once you say you are going to settle for second, that's what happens to you.

John F. Kennedy

Preparing for what we believe in will help develop additional leadership qualities. Even if we are perceived to not have what it takes to succeed, our ability to learn, grow, develop, and master the skills needed to be successful will eventually pay-off. Our inner strength should be our guide.

First they ignore you, then they laugh at you, then they fight you, then you win.

M.K. Gandhi

The upshot of being competitive is developing a drive to succeed. All the skill and talent of the world that is not put to use with zest will bring in only second-hand results.

Competitive spirit → Drive

Competitive spirit means staying one step ahead of the rest. Whether it means the innovation of a new product, delivering a new type of service, or getting the highest grades in school, we compete with the world every day. Competition is beneficial if its outcome is positive. Competing negatively defeats the very purpose of this attribute. The behavior should result in excellence when it forces us to do better.

An example of the positive effect of having a competitive spirit is that of "Pandora Radio." Many music providers stream songs over the internet, but Pandora Radio has taken the competitive spirit to new levels by delivering better and more customized songs than anyone else. It improves its offerings each day, striving to "wow" the customer. Best of all, the service receives its revenue from its sponsors, thus making it mostly free for users.

Competitive spirit generates excellence.

14. Ideas

Leaders get paid not so much for performing day-to-day tasks, but for their ideas. Ideas are the rich, organic mix of our vision for the future. Without them, businesses would very quickly run out of steam and be derailed. There would be no progress.

All achievements, all earned riches, have their beginning in an idea.

Napoleon Hill

How large should our idea be? That depends on us! There are no limits to dreaming and envisioning the products, services, and life of the future. Ideas are tax free too. Our potential is limitless.

Think big, believe big, act big, and the results will be big.

Anonymous

Many a new thought is lost because it is deemed to be too far-fetched or something that would not be practical or useful. Instead of discarding these thoughts, if we were to use them as springboards, they could eventually turn out to be game-changers.

All great deeds and all great thoughts have a ridiculous beginning.

Albert Camus

When an idea spreads and catches the imagination, there is no stopping it. We have seen that when people come together and share their dreams and inspirations, nothing can stop them.

No army can withstand the strength of an idea whose time has come.

Victor Hugo

Every vision springs from an idea. Intellectually stimulating our imagination leads to a desired state in the future.

Ideas lead to innovation. Star-Trek has long displayed ideas of speaking into a device pinned on a shirt to talk to someone remotely or the voice-activated requests made to a computer. These are now realities. Some of the other 'Trekkie" ideas, such as asking the computer to prepare a gourmet dish in minutes, or the ultimate, travel by beaming-over, are not here (yet), but one never knows when they could also become an everyday occurrence.

An idea is the seed of a future tree.

15. Problem Solving and Negotiation Skills

Winning in a competitive environment is possible by being adept at solving problems that lie in our way as roadblocks. If our problems are not resolved, it's difficult to be better than others. It takes a trained mind to solve them. In most cases, the approach used should be a disciplined one in which the root-cause is identified and fixed.

Focusing on a problem is good only to the extent of defining its severity and occurrence. Excessively dwelling on the problem will not solve it but could actually make it worse.

Identify your problems, but give your power and energy to solutions.

Anthony Robbins

Solving problems requires analytical skills. Extensive energy is spent in deriving solutions through calculations and theories. A simpler approach would be to show something concrete that everyone understands.

Few things are harder to put up with than the annoyance of a good example.

Mark Twain

Problem solving needs plenty of resources. It is not possible to fix the dent in a car with bare hands. Tools, coupled with the knowledge to use them, are needed to fix issues.

If the only tool you have is a hammer, you tend to see every problem as a nail.

Abraham Maslow

Problems occur when some things go wrong. The frame of mind that existed before the problem happened cannot be the same used to fix it. Solving problems needs a fresh look at the issues to arrive at creative solutions.

A problem cannot be solved with the same consciousness that created it.

Albert Einstein

In addition to problem solving, another way to lay the foundation for preparedness is by having negotiating skills that eliminate future roadblocks. A stalemate condition could take forever to get resolved, thus compromising readiness. Negotiations can lead to greater sales, better products, and even fewer wars. Making the other side see your point of view and you seeing theirs could fix a lot of our ills without the pain of enduring a protracted state of in-betweeness.

In quarrelling truth is always lost.

Syrus

Negotiations involve giving up some ground to gain others. What is ceded need not be less than what is obtained. Sometimes the act of giving can have long-lasting goodwill benefits.

Sacrifice remains the solution of that which has no solution.

Jean Guiton

The art of negotiation can directly help increase sales and revenues. Great deals have been struck and big treaties have been signed thanks to its powers.

In business, you don't get what you deserve. You get what you negotiate.

Chester L. Karrass

Ask and you shall receive. Try that with employers, employees, or anyone around you. Our ability to negotiate can yield great dividends if used well. The sky is the limit.

The reason why so little is done is generally because so little is attempted.

Samuel Smiles

Problem-solving and negotiating skills prepare us to seize opportunities. Once we are prepared, we can move ahead toward success.

Problem Solving
and Negotiation
Skills

Preparedness

In his book "Think and Grow Rich," Napoleon Hill advocates overcoming problems by thinking of the end-state and working backwards to eliminate the root of the problem. When faced with a difficult situation, we often do not know the correct path to its solution and have several options to consider, without knowing which one will work. If we were to reverse our thinking, visualize ourselves in the state where the issue is resolved and then map out what would have worked to be in that state, the solution becomes more obvious.

Visualize the end state and you'll find a way to get there.

16. Risk Taking

Risk taking is always talked about positively but only for its successes. All failures are orphans and are categorized as stupid mistakes. Successes have their blessings from "the ability to take risks" department and are also referred to as "calculated risks." Well, no one wants to glorify failure, but often the lessons we learn from a failed attempt are invaluable and can be used to accomplish something even greater in the future.

Nine out of ten of what we call new ideas are simply old mistakes.

G. K. Chesterton

Failure is a bad thing if only tried once. For someone who keeps on going forward, it could actually be good. It will provide quick learning and allow one to change direction if needed. As long as the farm is not lost in every unsuccessful attempt, failure could be a great research lab. It's the start of a long journey to success.

If you want to succeed, double your failure rate.

Tom Watson, Sr.

Success is a relative term. Just as there is no good without bad, so it is with success.

Success has no meaning without failure.

Anonymous

Success does not come free. It takes risk and effort to win.

The policy of being too cautious is the greatest risk of all.

Jawaharlal Nehru

There is a difference between taking risks and gambling. The odds for success vary greatly between the two. So, for all the good things said about risk taking, it has to be viewed through the lens of what was considered before taking the risk.

The difference between stupidity and genius is that genius has its limits.

Albert Einstein

Risk taking is not just a question of success or failure. It could also involve hardships and facing obstacles that we wouldn't normally expect.

When you go in search of honey, you must expect to be stung by bees.

Joseph Joubert

Some of the greatest motivators of all time have been the "nay-sayers." When someone dismisses our abilities, it's time to prove them wrong.

The great pleasure of life lies in doing what people say you cannot do.

Walter Bagehot

An over-cautious approach slows things down. An appetite for calculated and intuitive risk taking makes us move faster without getting dragged down by over-analyzing any situation.

A great story about risk taking can be recounted from the experience of Hewlett-Packard and its launch of the scientific calculator. All its marketing research showed was that no one would purchase a new machine called the "scientific calculator" for a thousand dollars. What HP decided to do was to take a measured risk and make about a thousand units to see if any of them would sell. To their surprise, everything that they placed on store shelves vanished before their eyes; and so did the next thousand; and so on. Nobody had predicted the runaway success of this device or that consumers would be ready to pay a hefty sum for it. HP's decision to take small risks in an incremental fashion while maintaining speed of action resulted in a success story.

Taking small, measured risks can result in big gains.

17. Results Oriented and Timeliness

Being results oriented is the core of doing business. This could include new product or service innovations, breakthroughs in marketing, customer satisfaction, or achieving new levels of excellence. The output we see today is due to the strategies and efforts of yesterday. In order to continue delivering profits, companies need to conceive new initiatives and actions each day to protect the future. With results come profits.

Don't judge each day by the harvest you reap, but by the seeds you plant.

Robert Louis Stevenson

Great results may or may not lead to great success. There are plenty of examples where people and companies accomplished excellent results but did not translate them into something more meaningful. On a more personal note, success should mean happiness and if it does not, the path was lost somewhere along the way.

There is only one success, to be able to spend your life in your own way.

Anonymous

At the end of the day, it's not the effort but the outcome that matters. If someone can deliver all the results with minimal input, so be it.

Don't tell me how hard to work, tell me how much to get done.

Ling

What we accomplish is to be cherished. It's emblazoned in our memory. The hours, days, weeks, months, and years spent with no output or outcome lie fallow in our memories, merging into one big block, but that small moment of victory lives on forever.

Remember that life is not measured in hours but in accomplishments.

James A. Pike

Results come from actions, which in-turn come from a variety of additional inputs. Inspiration is an important ingredient for action. Without it, no one would want to do much. It has to be sought after, found, and acquired.

When inspiration does not come to me, I go half way to meet it.

Sigmund Freud

Results need to be timely, otherwise their relevance is diminished. We have heard over the years that time and tide do not wait for anyone. If something is not accomplished within a given timeframe, its value is reduced. It's easy to pass time with excessive contemplation on what the fix should be. At some point, a decision needs to be made to move ahead and get the job done.

Short as life is, we make it still shorter by the careless waste of time.

Victor Hugo

Timeliness is compromised if one is focused on negatives and imperfections. We should make the most of what we know and use those strengths.

Do not let what you cannot do interfere with what you can do.

John Wooden

Timely results challenge us to reach out farther and push on boundaries that would not be initially visible. The concept of stretch goals is based on relying on our ability to deliver great results and use that to dramatically move the target.

Results and timeliness	→	Stretch

The value of results and timeliness is highlighted by General Motors when it delivered on the promise of the Volt, the first plug-in electric vehicle. The timing could not have been better, with the rising prices of oil and political instability around the world. Creating a new product or service that nobody needs could end up costing a company a lot of valuable resources. Need should drive innovation.

Timing is everything.

18. Decision Making

When decisions are not made and things are allowed to fester, there is ambiguity in the air. This state of transition makes people nervous. It is better to decide and move forward on a venture than to contemplate endlessly, trying to make sure that all parties get what they want.

It is, of course, impossible to please all the people all the time.

D. H. McCullaugh

Decisions need to be based on reality. It is fine to dream the dream, ideate, and innovate. But there is a point where dreams clash with reality and that's where being practical minded helps.

A wise man never attempts the impossible.

Phillip Massinger

Decisions are often based on "either-or" situations. After a decision is made, it is not possible to know what would have happened if a different path had been selected. We can always hypothesize and speculate, but we can never be sure.

It's not possible to go back in time and change an action, so we need to be confident in our selected path.

Two roads diverged in a wood and I –
I took the one less travelled by,
And that has made all the difference.

Robert Frost

Learning from past mistakes helps us avoid making them again. To take the same mis-step twice is like expecting a movie to have a different ending the next time we watch it.

Those who continue on the same path taken previously are either very comfortable with the way it's going or just haven't thought it through.

A well- adjusted person is one who makes the same mistake twice without getting nervous.

Jane Heard

Being decisive has great rewards. It also has its consequences. Decisions with bad results do not make a good conversation. Mistakes will happen, but we must try to minimize their impact, or to say it bluntly, make them less often.

No one can be right all of the time but it helps to be right most of the time.

Robert Half

Decision making could end up at odds with other management competencies, such as teamwork. If the final owner of the project thinks that his or her decision should override the team's consensus opinion, then there should be tremendous conviction in his or her thought and action.

I am extremely patient provided I get my way in the end.

Margaret Thatcher

All the decisions we make and priorities we set need to translate into success and allow us to reflect on our actions. Without the end results, these actions would not have much importance. Even failure is a form of success and should be used to improve decision making and priority setting.

Decision Making → Reflection, Wisdom & Success

The decision made by Wal-Mart to pull out of Germany in 2006 was not easy. It was a bitter pill to swallow for the world's largest retailer when it decided to sell all its stores to a local German company and incur a loss of about a billion dollars. Wal-Mart struggled from the start in a market of well-established retailers. The reasons for its failure were many, but contributing to it was its decision to impose an Americanized model in a different country, without regard to local culture. Germans were not very receptive to some of Wal-Mart's well intentioned mis-steps, such as offering to bag groceries for customers who preferred to do it themselves. They were also unsure of how to react to over-friendly smiling clerks at the checkout and would have been more comfortable with brusque checkout personnel.

Be aware of ground realities when making decisions.

19. Fairness, Empathy, and Talent Recognition

There is no system that can accomplish the goal of being one hundred percent fair to all. People's salaries and wages are based on their qualifications, experience, skill, and the value they bring to the table. Once that is determined, wages are typically fixed. At this point, the concept of fairness lies in the hands of both the employer and employee to make sure that work is creating the desired output.

You don't get paid for the hour. You get paid for the value you bring to the hour.

Jim Rohn

It takes deep insight to be fair. When we point out the mistakes of others, we may need to look at ourselves first to make sure we get the whole picture.

A truth not understood becomes error.

Desbarolles

We reap what we sow. When we give, our gift comes back in ways we cannot fathom. Our empathy for others will always be rewarded, if not in that instant, later in time.

Talk not of wasted affection; affection never was wasted.

Longfellow

As a result of practicing fairness and empathy, a lesser known, but great benefit that emerges is the ability to recognize pure talent. A lot of positions are filled because somebody knows someone. This approach works for the one who is selected, but does disservice to the larger talent bank. In order to truly excel in the future, an unbiased raw recognition of talent will reap great rewards for all.

Most people want to acquire talent, but few realize that much more can be accomplished by recognizing talent in others. Finding and selecting the right person for a job can be the difference between success and failure. One of the first steps in recognizing talent is to select someone with latent abilities and empower him or her to take the business forward.

Great people are those who make others feel that they too can become great.

Mark Twain

Another step in recognizing talent is to start by giving everyone the benefit of doubt. All should begin with a clean slate. It makes people want to excel.

I always prefer to believe the best of everybody. It saves so much trouble.

Rudyard Kipling

The world tolerates a lot from talented people. Whether it is specialist programmers working odd hours because they cannot come into work at regular times or top actors making the filming crew wait for of no apparent reason, talented people get away with a lot of negative attributes.

But then, having none of the negatives without any talent will not take us much farther.

It has been my experience that folks who have no vices have very few virtues.

Abraham Lincoln

Talent does not have to be perfect; nor does a leader. The vehicle used to make progress can have its blemishes, but its core should work solidly.

Usefulness is not impaired by imperfection. You can drink from a chipped cup.

Greta K. Nagel

It is surprising how the qualities of being fair, showing empathy, and recognizing talent lead to success. The ability to succeed is usually attributed to concrete actions and the softer human side is not given enough credit in reaching the goal.

| Fairness, Empathy & Talent Recognition | | Reflection, Wisdom & Success |

Fairness and empathy lead to recognizing talent. It does not take a trained eye to see that around the world a lot of hiring and promotions occur without much regard to the actual talent of the candidate. When real talent is the only consideration, the results speak for themselves. There have been several companies in which the CEOs have started at the bottom of the ladder and moved all the way up based on only one criterion, their talent. Here, the credit goes not only to the ones who made it to the top, but also to those who recognized them in the most unbiased manner.

Talent and ability are difficult for anyone to ignore for too long.

20. Drive

Drive drives the world. If we lost our passion for accomplishments, we would stagnate and regress.

As long as I have a want, I have a reason for living. Satisfaction is death.

George Bernard Shaw

If it's broken, fix it. Don't cry over it. Drive gives us the ability to improve on what needs attention. A lackadaisical approach will result in no output. With drive, we can focus on our strengths and work on change.

The remedy for weakness is not brooding over weakness, but thinking about strength.

Vivekananda

As we succeed, we keep building on what we have done to create our output. It is only failure that allows us to reboot. As much as we all hate failure, it is the only mechanism that makes us rethink and retool.

Failure is only the opportunity to more intelligently begin again.

Henry Ford

We don't need to be geniuses to get things done. What we do is based on the drive and will to succeed. That will lead us to the path of preparedness and action. The world is replete with examples of those who knew a lot, but did nothing with their knowledge.

Nothing is more humiliating than to see idiots succeed in enterprises we have failed in.

Samuel Johnson

Drive impacts performance. If we are motivated to succeed and perceive our ability to be the best, chances are that we will accomplish our goals. Results are based on willpower.

The way you see yourself today will affect your performance today.

Zig Ziglar

The drive to succeed does not develop in a closed environment. Our thinking has brought us to this point in time when our progress has exploded exponentially. What was considered magical not too long ago is now real.

Minds are like parachutes: they only function when open.

Thomas R. Dewar

Drive causes us to be prepared for future challenges. The better the preparation, the more serendipitous the circumstances will be.

I am a strong believer in luck and I find the harder I work the more I have of it.

Benjamin Franklin

No business can afford to stand still. If we are not thinking of innovating or launching new products and services in the future, we could find ourselves obsolete in a very short time. The goal is to move as fast as possible to keep the competition at bay.

Business is like riding a bicycle. You won't fall off unless you stop pedaling.

Claude Pepper

The drive to succeed is embedded in the philosophy that win or lose things are being done for the right reasons.

Confidence comes not from always being right but from not fearing to be wrong.

Peter T. McIntyre

Drive is a key enabler of success. It should also be a motivator to reflect on success.

The best place to observe drive is among students. Some want to go over and above, others are satisfied with doing the minimum required, while the rest are not interested in complying with anything. Those who have the drive to do more push harder to venture into new areas, thus breaking traditional boundaries and delivering beyond what was expected.

Drive is the engine of success.

21. Vision

Each one of us should have our vision for the future. This vision could be a new and innovative product or service, the way things work, how we plan to grow our business or self worth, or even the way we think. We should all define our vision and make it our goal to accomplish it.

A vision could be a simple thought, but the actions needed to accomplish it are often lengthy and tedious. A world without violence, mutual respect for one another at the workplace, or a product that can solve world hunger: all are simple statements but none is easy to accomplish.

The point of the vision is that there can be no grand future without thinking of it. Vision should be a driver behind our motivations.

We've got to have a dream if we are going to make a dream come true.

Denis Waitley

A vision is a place we want to be in the future. It is not a fantasy. It should be attainable, even if it seems far-fetched or like reaching for the moon.

We must learn our limits. We are something, but none of us is everything.

Blaise Pascal

The main idea of a vision is in its belief that it will be reality someday.

Trust in dreams, for in them is the hidden gate of eternity.

Khalil Gibran

Vision gets our sub-conscious mind working. What we envision for ourselves has a very high probability of becoming real.

Our minds, bodies and actions work in cohesion when they strive to accomplish a common goal.

Your imagination is the preview of life's coming attractions.

Albert Einstein

We are impacted by the extent of our current thinking.

What we see depends on where we are standing.

Robert McAfee

Vision's correlation with success cannot be more emphasized. It does not have much use if created in a vacuum but when mixed with other ingredients, it will form a potent mixture and will eventually be accomplished.

At many companies, the vision is a statement mainly used for slogans and banners. It usually conjures up images of being the very best in what the company does. Not a bad idea, but if all its stakeholders do not embrace the vision as if it were their own, its relevance is greatly diminished. A vision statement becomes true if all involved believe in it. The employees should be its ambassadors and should see it in action every day at work. This task is not easy, but if someone at the top can figure out how to do it, he or she can unleash the power of a team to accomplish great heights of success.

Make the vision relevant.

22. Preparedness

The motto of being prepared does not apply only to the scouts. Great opportunities are missed if we are not prepared to take advantage of them. What use is it to be a bystander while someone else gets the next big order? Anticipating change can help us prepare for the future. If due diligence is done with strategy and plans and appropriate resources are expended, we can be first in line when opportunity comes knocking.

In the field of observation, chance favors only the prepared mind.

Louis Pasteur

Being ready for the next project requires a lot of work and preparation.

People always call it luck when you have acted more sensibly than they have.

Anne Tyler

Getting started is half done. Being present will take us over three quarters of the way.

Opportunity dances for those who are already on the dance floor

Jackson Brown

One of the key reasons people and companies fail to be fully prepared is that they get swayed by the good fortunes of their times. We do not have to look back very far when basics such as food and water were considered a luxury.

We take things for granted, almost with a sense of entitlement. It's in these good times that we should prepare for the worst.

When you are fortunate, beware of adversity.

Anonymous

The time invested in getting prepared yields results at the end. Most people are impatient and want to see the result of their work quickly. It's the next quarterly statement or the next meeting that's important. How about looking at the big picture, understanding what is the most critical to accomplish, and going about preparing for it?

If I had eight hours to chop down a tree, I'd spend six sharpening my axe.

Abraham Lincoln

Preparedness should not have its limits. At work or at home, be ready for the worst while working toward getting the best.

There cannot be a crisis next week. My schedule is already full.

Henry Kissinger

Luck may favor the brave, but it is more partial to the prepared. Hard work coupled with good choices will lead to winning the proverbial lottery.

I find that the harder I work the more luck I seem to have.

Thomas Jefferson

Getting tough and being prepared are the best solutions to tackling anything that may come our way. No need to hope for the easy path when we are well prepared.

Don't ask for a light load, but rather ask for a strong back.

Anonymous

Those who are not ready to face the music tend to move to the background and watch the world go by. Those who are prepared take challenges head-on to be successful.

The world is full of willing people; some willing to work, the rest willing to let them.

Robert Frost

Life's lessons cannot be learned in a classroom. They have to be imbibed through experience and the school of hard-knocks.

Education is an admirable thing, but it is well to remember from time to time that nothing that is worth knowing can be taught.

Oscar Wilde

We should not make the mistakes our parents made; we should only make new ones if we have to. Being prepared includes not repeating something that we know does not work.

Is there anyone so wise as to learn from the experience of others?

Voltaire

Preparedness is probably one of the most difficult of the attributes that lead to success because it is the one that requires the most amount of hard-work without any guarantee if it will be worth it.

Preparedness → **Reflection, Wisdom & Success**

When the financial crisis came to the U.S. in 2008, it impacted most industries, but U.S.-based automotive companies were hit the hardest due to years of legacy practices that reduced their productivity and profitability. Of the "big three," Ford was able to weather the economic storm the best because of actions it had taken to prepare for the worst. This act of preparing for the worst and working toward accomplishing the best served Ford well in getting through the biggest economic crisis in recent memory.

Be prepared.

23. Speed

Speed is the rate at which an organization works. It is how fast we progress toward our stated goals. Speed is critical when there are competitive pressures and we want to be the first to market or wish to resolve customer-related problems quickly. Speed has its downsides too. It creates a state of flux and could also throw caution to the wayside. It's a great approach to progress when those guiding it are fully aware of its ramifications.

If everything seems under control, you're just not going fast enough.

Anonymous

The adage "slow and steady wins the race" might have been true at one time but now it's more like "fast and steady gets to the finish-line first." Moving with speed but not completing the race like the proverbial hare will not satisfy our fast-paced approach to progress. The tortoise has a lot more competitors now than it had previously.

One can never consent to creep when one has the impulse to soar.

Helen Keller

With progress comes the next challenge to push our boundaries farther. If we find ourselves fixing the same issues, having speed would not be very fruitful. Problems need to be fixed permanently. Innovation must take root.

The measure of success is not whether you have a tough problem to deal with, but whether it's the same problem you had last year.

John Foster Dulles

Another element of speed is effective communication. A lot is lost in translation if words and deeds are not clear. Effective communication can bag contracts, motivate people, or even win wars. It is the window to solutions and should be used in a manner that gets results.

Communication requires someone else at the other end. It cannot be done in isolation.

Everything in the world we want to do or get done, we must do with and through people.

Earl Nightingale

Business today is based on the dictum of faster and better. While there is something to be said for speed, there aren't too many advocates for the wait and watch approach.

Patience is the companion of wisdom.

St. Augustine

Speed not only gets to success quickly, but also eliminates a lot of extraneous activities.

| Speed | → | Reflection, Wisdom & Success |

Speed could be a direct contributor to success. If coordinated well with results and timeliness, it can help us beat the competition to the finish line. The example of the iPad coming out ahead of the rest in delivering a tablet computing system shows how speed made it the market leader. While the followers fought it out for the second spot, the iPad was miles ahead of its competitors.

The fastest players gain the opportunity to perfect themselves and be the best.

24. Stretch

Timely results can be further enhanced with stretch targets. Small gains are good to have but will not take one far. It is the stretch in the results that make all the difference - something that goes beyond expectations, more than what could have been done. Each person has his or her own perception of stretch.

We all live under the same sky but we don't all have the same horizon.

Konrad Adenauer

We get what we ask for. If we don't fully understand our potential, we will undersell ourselves and get only what others think our worth is. If we don't aim for the best, someone else will, since we did not even try.

My Wage

**"I bargained with Life for a penny,
And Life would pay no more,**

However I begged at evening
When I counted my scanty store.

For Life is a just employer,
He gives you what you ask,
But once you have set the wages,
Why, you must bear the task.

I worked for a menial's hire,
Only to learn, dismayed,
That any wage I had asked of Life,
Life would have willingly paid."

Jessie B. Rittenhouse

We may feel that we are at the forefront of progress, battling the unknown and facing challenges never experienced before. The fact, though, is that those who came before us have faced challenges that far exceed what we see today.

Here is the secret to inspiration. Tell yourself that thousands and tens of thousands of people, not very intelligent and certainly no more intelligent than the

**rest of us, have mastered problems as
difficult as those that now baffle you.**

William Feather

Stretch makes success better with more than what
was initially planned for.

The website "Innocentive.com" is an example of
where the concept of stretch comes to life.
Challenges are opened up daily for participants to
compete against one another and deliver the best
solution for a problem or issue. People from all
over the world participate to invent and discover
something new.

Stretch goals lead to new boundaries.

25. Success

Success is a state of mind. It is not a race to see who will die the richest, who will have the most market share, or whose stock price will gain the most. Success is happiness and well-being packaged together.

Success is liking yourself, liking what you do, and liking how you do it.

Maya Angelou

It is ironic to see businesses flourish on the balance-sheet but be in a state of disarray when it comes to day-to-day operations. Employees working for these companies would not consider themselves to be successful.

No concept of success can be divorced from peace of mind.

Alving H. Goeser

Success has a million parents, but failure is an orphan. The reasons for failure are many and often times very legitimate. These reasons, although true, could have been approached with different solutions. It's time we took ownership of our actions and fix them.

We have forty million reasons for failure, but not a single excuse.

Rudyard Kipling

Go for the gold. Any Olympian will affirm that their target was not the silver or the bronze medal. They practice to win first spot.

Aim at heaven and you get earth thrown in; aim at earth and you get neither.

C. S. Lewis

The road to success is strewn with signs of failure at every turn. Drivers have the option to stop, or to just continue doing their best with intrinsic motivation.

Success is going from failure to failure without losing enthusiasm.

Winston Churchill

Success is not just an accident. It is the result of a well-envisioned plan that comes to fruition after hard work and dedication. The first step toward success is to imagine the end-state and then diligently start working to accomplish it.

Whatever the mind can conceive and believe, the mind can achieve.

Napoleon Hill

If you build it, they will come. Many a time we are amazed at the success of products and services that most experts thought should not be in the market.

Success has a simple formula: do your best and people may like it.

Sam Ewing

Success isn't final. It is a temporary landing station, used to launch the next phase of a journey. At no time should people or a business be so fully satisfied that they have no motivation to move ahead further.

Show me a thoroughly satisfied person and I'll show you a failure

Thomas Edison

What most people considered impossible in the past is commonplace today. Talking picture frames, wireless communication, 3-D simulation; all would be the miracles of yesteryear.

It is difficult to say what is impossible, for the dream of yesterday is the hope of today and the reality of tomorrow.

Robert Goddard

Success is not a static condition. Meshed with time, it requires hard work just to sustain it, let alone making it better. It is a moving target that needs constant attention to prevent complacency from creeping in without anybody realizing it.

I dread success. To have succeeded is to have finished one's business on earth, like the male spider, who is killed by the female the moment he has succeeded in his courtship. I like the state of continued becoming, with a goal in front and not behind.

George Bernard Shaw

Results alone do not matter in the end. It's what we do with those results. Being rich could be a result but working for the betterment of society is more like success. Giving back, not just in cash and kind, but in the form of service, innovation, and even business constitutes success.

To do more for the world than the world does for you – that is success.

Henry Ford

Success and reflection go hand-in-hand.

Tony Hsieh joined Zappos as the CEO in 1999 and then doubled revenues every year. In July 2009 Amazon.com announced the acquisition of Zappos in a deal valued at approximately 1.2 billion US dollars. Selling shoes on the internet did not seem as a venture that would have any legs, but with Tony's approach of "Delivering Happiness," what Zappos did was more than just sell shoes. Its culture of ensuring that both, employees and customers feel really good paid off in a big way. This is because Hsieh concluded that his entire business revolved around one thing: happiness. Everything at Zappos served that single end. By motivating and energizing its employees and transferring that same good feeling to customers, Zappos brought success to its feet!

Success is simplicity.

26. Reflection and Wisdom

Reflection ties-in all the leadership traits talked about so far. Actions taken by leaders need to be evaluated for their value and meaning. It's the speed to bring to market, the first mover advantage, and the ability to constantly innovate that drives organizations. This continual push-ahead is good and keeps us moving but every once in a while it is worth reflecting on our path. It would be sad to be caught in an evolutionary trap of the dinosaur. Reflecting will reap great benefits and allow us to select the way that will not end in regrets.

Much silence and a good disposition, there are no two things better than these.

Prophet Mohammed

We typically get involved in our day-to-day lives, managing each event as it comes by. However, if we do not nourish our sense of adventure, we will not have the satisfaction of doing things and learning life's lessons. Missed opportunities do not make bestselling books or movies.

If you don't have good stories to tell at your deathbed, what good was living?

Jennifer Tilly

The definition of success and failure is set and measured by society. We need to look at it not from other people's point of view, but from our own lens.

There is no defeat except from within.

Elbert Hubbard

Leadership is not all centered around materialism. It should reach our more noble thoughts.

Generosity is giving more than you can and pride is taking less than you need.

Khalil Gibran

Pride and ego are the greatest enemies of not only the rich and famous, but also the smart and intelligent. All too often these traits get in the way of learning something valuable that could be used for our benefit. Even our biggest enemy or the worst boss will teach us something worth learning.

The greatest lesson in life is to know that even fools are right sometimes.

Winston Churchill

There is nothing more easily available than free advice. It's all around us; we may be guilty of doling it out too. If only we did what we tell others to do, we would have the perfect parents, bosses, politicians and world leaders.

The best way to succeed in life is to act on the advice you give to others.

Anonymous

Happiness and sadness are a state of mind, a function of our surroundings, and are even part of our evolution. These perceptions drive our behavior and actions.

We choose our joys and sorrows long before we experience them.

Khalil Gibran

Even the best times are never realized in the moment. We need a comparison with bad ones to realize the good. Happiness is relative and if we find ourselves worrying about the insignificant, that's a clue that we are really happy.

We are never happy; we can only remember that we once were.

Alexander Smith

Adversity is unfortunate and may have a long-lasting impact on our lives. In spite of this, we should be positive and change with new realities.

Living is the art of getting used to what we didn't expect.

Eleanor Wood

Happiness cannot be pursued. It should be a by-product of actions taken to follow dreams. In that sense, it is a follower, not a leader.

The search for happiness is one of the chief sources of unhappiness.

Eric Hoffer

Happiness is intrinsic. External stimuli can make us laugh, smile, or even cry, but happiness is felt in ways others cannot see.

It is not easy to find happiness in ourselves, and it is not possible to find it elsewhere.

Agnes Repplier

Reflection is putting things in perspective, not getting caught in the heat of the moment and looking at the big picture. It forms the root of our work, lives and priorities.

We build memories each day and love to relive our good experiences many times over. To have the pleasure to reflect on some key points in time and feel great about oneself is an exhilarating experience.

To be able to look back on one's life with satisfaction is to have lived twice.

Khalil Gibran

Wisdom is to know that all our delights, opportunities, disappointments, and changes are transient. We need to make sure that we focus on having a good time while we can since we can't predict what comes next.

There is no cure for birth and death save to enjoy the interval.

George Santayana

Modern business management emphasizes speed and action but in the bargain, has forgotten some gems of wisdom that have stood the test of time and will never let anyone down. Although much maligned in today's fast paced world, not taking any action can be extremely strategic and results-oriented. It takes the right person to recognize and understand these abilities.

All human wisdom is summed up in two words - wait and hope.

Alexandra Dumas

Decision making helped by the quality of wisdom greatly improves our chances of success.

Wisdom is the ability to make decisions that work-out for the best in the long run. It does not take a short-term view of what we do. When Vonage decided to give free international calling from the U.S. to over sixty countries, it was not an instant hit. The idea took time to percolate and spread through the many ethnic communities that were initially skeptical of this offer. With word-of-mouth and a long-term strategy, Vonage was able to win over many new customers who began to see value in its service.

Reflection determines whether the success gained was worth the effort. It also helps us decide if the path being chosen is going to develop on what has already been gained or take us in the opposite direction. Over the years we have seen companies reach dizzy heights only to find out later that a lot of the good initial work was followed by dubious decisions to show the world that all was well.

Enron is a prime example of success gone haywire. After building up a legitimate multi-national company, a few people at the top decided to hoodwink all their stakeholders into believing that things were continuing to go well when in-fact, they were not. A bit of reflection at this point would have truly helped those who thought that they should deceive others to look good in the moment. All actions have consequences and Enron was no exception.

Think before you act.

About the Author

Yusuf Biviji is an automotive and telecommunications professional with extensive industry knowledge. He holds advanced degrees in both Engineering and Business Administration. Over the past seventeen years, his experiences have spanned several areas of business that have inspired him to reflect on leadership and what drives it. These thoughts are outlined in this book. If you have any comments or feedback regarding its contents, you may contact him at ybiv01@yahoo.com.

Notes